Beast

between
y and
edom.
old age,
two-
his own
st in love,
resents
and
s, until
izure of
vorld,
ide of

by the same author

THE PLAY OF WILLIAM COOPER AND EDMUND DEW-NEVETT

other Methuen Playscripts

A Methuen Playscript

The Two-Backed Beast

DAVID SELBOURNE

First published in Great Britain 1969
by Methuen & Co Ltd
11 New Fetter Lane London EC4
Copyright © 1969 by David Selbourne

Set by Tina Fisker
5 Kingsbury Road London N1
Printed by Redwood Press Ltd
Trowbridge Wiltshire

The Two-Backed Beast was first staged at the Everyman Theatre, Liverpool on December 4, 1968 with the following cast:

SAMUEL	Norman Florence
MILLY, his daughter	Alison Fiske
BILLY, his son	Anthony Boden
JACK	Sam Kelly
and the two-backed beast	
JAMES	Bill Stewart
MARTHA	Gillian Hanna
HARRY, the accordion player	Henry Salter

GUESTS AND CUSTOMERS

Directed by Peter James

For my Father and Mother

Act One

SCENE ONE

Kindly, genial, nimble SAMUEL, lord of his long–lived–in–
domain, stands before a flickering fire. There are sounds
of conversation off–stage.

He is rubicund, agile, and greying prematurely. He has
just eaten in a neighbouring room.

He belches and rubs his belly; then sits down, at ease,
scratching and picking his nose.

SAMUEL: Oh! Ah!
          Ah!
          Ooh!
          Eee!
          Chi..ildren!
          Dadd..y ...wants you!

(Two children enter: a YOUTH of about sixteen, and a
GIRL, almost a woman, of about seventeen; they are
both dressed in page–boy hotel uniforms.)

          Have you forgotten, kiddies, eh?
          Daddy wants his little spit–spit, kiddywinkies!

          Get it!!
          How can you forget? Again!
          Eh?
          Your poor Daddy! You never think, do you?
          Eh?

(Exeunt CHILDREN, SAMUEL laughing. The YOUTH
returns with a white handkerchief, the GIRL with a brass
spittoon, covered with a cloth. They perform according
to known rules and manoeuvres. He spits into spittoon;
the handkerchief is presented.)

          Ust! Ah! Mm! Hm!
          Thank you, darling!
          Lovely girl!
          Take it, take it! Lad!!

(Exeunt CHILDREN, in step.)

          Ah!
          Poor kids!
          They don't know any better.

They forget the routines. They're only human.

Kids! They'll grow up.
They'll understand me.
That'll be the day.
We'll be friends, truly.

Give me advice, help me out, friendship and so
on.
Beautiful! Dream-like!
More harmony, more understanding,
Everything so nice, and orderly.

They give me trouble now, but what can you do?
They're good children.

(Crying off-stage.)

And they cry!

(Dancing.)

And look at me!
They cry!
The cheek!!
But wait till they see what I've got for them!
Won't they be surprised?
Ye..es!
Not yet, mind you.
Keep it back, do it slowly.

Gently, gently Samuel goes, on his little tip-
toes.
That's my policy. Always wait for the right
moment!!

(A pause. Distant thunder. SAMUEL chucklin):

Sammy and his set of rules!

(SAMUEL sits down.)

Don't they get annoyed!
That's kids for you!
Still, everything's all right.
Security!
Comfort!
Love!!
Ah. If only I'd had their luck.

(A pause.)

> My 'little set of values!!'
> They get cross!
> My god, yes, they do, certainly they do!
> And how!!
> Wheeee!!

(Distant thunder.)

> A storm coming!
> Do they have to fear? I ask you.
> Warmth! A roof over their heads!
>
> You're enjoying yourselves, aren't you, chil-
>   dren?!!

(Distant thunder.)

> Course they are. They're only kids, after all.
> Yes...es! It's OK here, basically.
>
> Sure!!

(Crying off-stage.)

SCENE TWO

The same place. It is morning, a bright day.
The GIRL quickly dusts, straightens.
The YOUTH carries in coal, and places it on the fire.

They wear their uniforms.

As they dart out, both carrying lists, which they check,
as they go, in runs SAMUEL, breathless, dapper, pow-
dered, smartened, excited.

SAMUEL: Little do they know, so little!
         The young innocents. Today's the day.
         Oh, whoopee! A day for daring.
         A delight for them, so charming.

(Enter the YOUTH, carrying a double wooden chair, two-
backed.)

> That's it. Well-made. Perfect!
> No! No! There! Round a bit. Good, good.
> Ooh!
> Next, next!! Quick! Item three!

> Good boy!
> Run!!

(Exit the YOUTH, passing the GIRL; she carries a water-jug, and runs to a vase, bearing a few flowers.)

> Water, water!
> Magnificent!
> No! No! Don't!!
> Not their pretty heads!!
> The dears! Gently to the stalks, child, run the
> bubbling liquid down!

> There, there!
> Better!
> Off you go, girlie!!
> Lovely, lovely girl!

(Exit GIRL.)

> Aaah. All set.
> Now!
> The moment we've all been waiting for,
> This is it, this could be the moment.

(Looking at pocket-watch.)

> All the way from foreign parts, the piece of
> resistance, the last word in entertainment, and
> replete with diverting possibilities, I introduce
> ...sure...

(A music-hall pose, dancing.)

> ...the one and only, or rather two and only,
> double-backed beast, sensation of the occident,
> envy of the solitary...

(Another pose, a hop and skip.)

> ...Unique in a divided world---that's it, that's
> the word for it...that'll do fine...

(The joined two-armed, two-backed, four legged twin BEAST enters unseen, shambling, each arm carrying a small pack. SAMUEL strikes another pose, his back to the beast.)

> ENTER!!
> ...Any second, any moment...
> ...This'll liven the kiddies up, all for them,
> their old papa's last trick, before I go, they'll
> be grateful, such a surprise, O such a sur-
> prise I'll give them, oh, this'll keep 'em
> moving, they'll be sorry, will they be sorry!

I bring life to them; they lack for nothing!
Oh, ow, COME ON!!!
...WHERE ARE THEY?!!!

Oh! Agh!
Yes!
Here!
You're here! Nice journey?

On time, just on time. Ha!
Good, good.
All perfect.
You must be Jack and James!
Good names!
They fit the...two of you; it's quite uncanny.

(Shaking hands):

Pleased...to meet you. Yes. How'd you do?
Hope you'll...er...
...fit in...to...how d'you do?
...our...household...and its routines.

We're...a happy family.
All compact. A bit dull, maybe. Not very
                    adventurous, maybe.
Till now. Ha, ha!

Yes. Put your bags or packs down.
I'll call the...children...my kiddies...
Such lovely children, real beauties.

(Shouting):

Kiddies!!! A surprise!

(Whispering):

Come and see your nice surprise!

(A pause.)

They're here now.

(Silence.)

It's only a small world you've come to. Mind
  you, we're trying to...expand, gents slowly...
I mean, not everyone would take you in, would
                    they?
Oh dear, what am I saying?
The ramblings of a dotard.
Don't protest! I know, I know.
I don't...feel young, that's all.
Heart! Ticker! Unsafe!

Sitting on a volcano!
Angor animi, the doc says.
Troubled soul, a troubled soul.
Looked it up, I'm a reader.
Still, glad to be here to greet you.
You never know, in the twinkling of an eyelid...

(Softly):

...Children!

We'll be friends, uh?
Stick together?
I'm sorry.
We'll all be attached to each other!
Oh dear, what am I saying?
I'm very sensitive. Oh god, yes.
Still I'm innocent. You can see that.

I'm innocent, basically; of course you can see
that.

You can't take offence then, can you, gents?
If I'm not guilty, eh, heh-heh!

(A pause.)

Yes..what was I saying?
Our own small world here...and our way of
doing things, and so on and so forth.
You'll get to know it, you're bound to.
Everything has a reason.
No universal poses here, though,
No grand statements.
The kiddies will explain it.

It's small, but intimate.
Our own taste, our own creation.

That's what a family's for, isn't it?
You'll fit in, gents, you'll make it.
Just a little adjustment'll be needed.
I'm sure you'll manage,
One way or the other.

(He belches, or farts, then scratches anxiously.)

Wait till you meet them!
Maybe they're coming. O god, they're coming.
Silly-billies! Wait a moment!
Hey! Let's give them a fright, boys, shall we?
Listen!

(He seizes the BEASTS, and whispers.)

                    What a plan! Eh?
                    Hide! Quickly! Quickly!!

(Exit, the TWO-BACKED BEAST.)

                    Shoo, shoo! Ha, ha!
                    There! That's it! All right?
                    Children!!

(To himself):

                    They're here now!

(To audience):

                    My kiddies can take all sorts, you know!
                    I've trained 'em. Heh, heh.

(Enter BILLY and MILLY. He backs away.)

BILLY: ...What do you want?
          You knew we were busy.

SAMUEL: I've got a surprise for you.
          Hm?
          You like a surprise? Hm?
          Billy? Milly?

MILLY: Tell us what it is then!

SAMUEL: ...I have a surprise...
          ...Really...

                    ...For you only...

BILLY: Well? What is it?

SAMUEL: ...Er...er...later.
          It's not the right moment. Eh?
          Billy! Milly!
          I wanted to warn you, that's all, in case of...
          ...It was only...

(A pause.)

                    ...Teh! Oh!
                    A shame!
                    Aaah!

                    Couldn't do it!
                    Why not, eh, coward?

(A pause. Shouting):

                    It wasn't the right moment!! That's all!!

(To the BEASTS):

                    Poor creatures!!

I've let you down, haven't I?!!
Eh? Tell me, tell me!!!

(JACK and JAMES reappear; BILLY and MILLY recoil,
open-mouthed, clinging to each other.)

SCENE THREE

The same place. Standing still, centre, backs to
audience, are JACK and JAMES, now uniformed, a
little proud.

JACK: Another garb, eh?

JAMES: In livery!

   (They chuckle together.)

JACK: A vulgarian this one, don't you think?

JAMES: Can't be helped.

   (They shuffle towards the fire.)

JACK: He'll make a joke of us. I feel it.

JAMES: Maybe.

JACK: A joke.

JAMES: A charade?

JACK: An entertainment. I can tell.

JAMES: Maybe.

JACK: Don't 'maybe' the whole time!

JAMES: Sorry, sorry.

JACK: Why be so dull, eh?

JAMES: Me? It's you. Not me.

JACK: Here we go!

JAMES: We're in livery, brother! Aren't you proud?
           Puff out your chest.
           Let's put our best feet forward!

JACK: Ah! The same old stuff.

JAMES: I'm trying...

JACK: ...to cheer us up, eh?
           The same old stuff. As I said.

(JACK walks, annoyed; JAMES too, pulled.)

>Don't get in a huff.
>You're so abrupt these days.
>You don't move like you used to.
>You hurt me, you know, often. Selfishness, that's
>>all.
>
>I never tell you.

JACK: Weakling!

JAMES: We're all right here. Eh?
>It feels right here doesn't it?
>Tell me!

JACK: Right?

JAMES: Safe. Comfortable.
>Hm?

JACK: Perhaps.

JAMES: 'Perhaps', eh?

(Gently):

>Now you, funny man...brother.
>
>Uniform fits: smart.
>Is yours all right, Jacko?

JACK: I expect so.

(JAMES looks at the joining section, pulling at it.)

JAMES: Good stitching for a change.
>She did it well.

(Pause.)

>She was a bit afraid of us, wasn't she, really?

(Pause.)

>Good girl, nice girl.
>Do you think she likes us?

JACK (bitterly):
>She has her orders, that's all. She has no choice!

(Copying SAMUEL):

>Smile, Milly, smile Milly, smile Milly!!!

JAMES: Poor girl.
>She served us, didn't she?
>That girl! Beautiful, pretty girl!
>
>Did she...touch you?

JACK: Fool!

JAMES: She did me. Brushed my hand across. Dear
                              scared girl!

JACK: Dreams!

JAMES: Made me shiver!

JACK: I didn't feel it.

JAMES: It was private.

JACK: Oh yes!

(A pause.)

JAMES: I'm inventing it.

JACK: Course. After all this time...like this, do you
                              still think you can kid me?

JAMES: I can. I have often.

JACK: You have not.

JAMES: Often.

JACK: Have you?

JAMES: No! I'm joking.

(A pause.)

JACK: We'll have to entertain them.

JAMES: Yes

(Giggling):

                              He'll be farting his way in soon, Jacko.

(They giggle and caper about, doing a soft-shoe shuffle.)

BOTH (singing and dancing):
                    'With a belch and a fart –
                    And a clutch at the heart –
                    Here comes Sammy,
                    Poor old Sammy,
                    Dear old Sammy,
                    Poor old Sammy
                    Long live Sammy,
                    And his...great...big...

JAMES: FART!!

JACK: HEART!!

BOTH: Sssh!

JAMES: They might be listening.

JACK: We're sovereign!

JAMES: Now who's dreaming?

JACK: Sovereigns inside...

JAMES: So you always say.

JACK: Prove I'm not!

JAMES: Prove you are!

JACK: I can't!

JAMES: Don't say it then!
          We're one! We're one!
          Don't say it!
          We're one! We're one!
          Don't spoil it.
          It's no use saying it.

JACK: All right! All right!
          I don't mean it.

JAMES: Why say it?
          Cheapjack!
          Skate!

JACK: All right!
          Don't let them hear us, friend!
          They might be listening!

JAMES: Yes, sorry, sorry.

JACK: Let's...run through it, hm?
          In case?
          Right?
          One...two...three...
          Nice...

JAMES: Uniform.

JACK: Isn't...

JAMES: ...It?

(They execute a rhythmic flourish.)

JACK: Quicker! Nice...

JAMES: ...Uniform...

JACK: ...Isn't...

JAMES: ...It?

JACK: Aren't we...

JAMES: ...Lucky...

JACK: ...To be...

JAMES: ...Here...

JACK: ...In your...

JAMES: ...Company?

JACK: Patter, quick. One...two...

JAMES: Why do we have...

JACK: ...Four eyes...

JAMES: ...When two...

JACK: ...Will do?...

JAMES: ...Why do we have...

JACK: ...Two hearts...

JAMES: ...When one...

JACK: ...Will do?

JAMES: Oh, why do we have...

JACK: Two minds –

JAMES: We don't!

JACK: We do! –

JAMES: When one...

JACK: ...Will do?!!!
          Do you think they'll like it?

JAMES: Of course.
          Let's try the new one, eh?
          One...two...

JACK (dancing):
          ...We...suffer in stolid patience...

JAMES: ...Examining...consolations...

(They stumble.)

BOTH: For our state!!!

JACK: Terrible! Again!! One...two...

JAMES: We suffer in stolid patience...

(Enter, SAMUEL, unseen, awakened from a nap, eye-wiping: in vest and trousers, without shoes.)

JAMES: ...Examining consolations!!

JACK: Examining consolations!!!

BOTH: ...For our state!!

SAMUEL: Settling down, boys?
          Everything all right? OK?

(With great agility, JACK and JAMES turn.)

JACK: ...Yes, sir!

(JACK tries to bow, tugging JAMES.)

SAMUEL: You feel at home? I'm sure you...

JAMES: ...Part of the family, sir, we are part of...

SAMUEL: ...Part? Part? What do you mean, 'part'?
          You do! Ah!

(A pause.)

        Marvellous.
        All my life, I wanted to have a nice place.
        For my children.
        I wanted to give them the best, only.
        Show them the world in all its teeming variety.
        Bring them the multiplicity of creation!

        Explain the mystery of the world!
        Exhibit god's order!
        Show them the wisdom and contrivance in all
                            things...

        ...In the natural...and the unnatural.
        Everything a beautiful...how shall I say?...
                            unit.

        Hm?
        I know what you think in your heart of hearts!
        The ravings of a simple man, eh?
        Yes?

(They shake their heads.)

        They are!
        My own thoughts.

(Tapping head vigorously):

        In here.
        The visions of Samuel, old King Samuel.
        Who would believe it?
        Here Samuel, and his children, and his...
                   guests, are safe!

        Eh?
        All the world goes down, but here is an island!
        No?

JACK: An asylum, a veritable asylum.

SAMUEL: Asylum??!
What do you mean, asylum?

JAMES: We mean a place of refuge, sir.

SAMUEL: Yes, oh, yes. I see.
Don't call me 'sir'.
A place of refuge.
Yes. Beautiful. Don't call me 'sir'!!
A refuge.
For the stricken and lonely, like me, eh?
For the sick and tired.

(SAMUEL walks slowly round them.)

You're very lucky! Ye...es!
Shall I tell you why?
Here!
Let Sammy tell!
You don't get lonely, do you?
Eh? Ha, ha, ha.

You got company.
You got each other. Ha, ha, ha!

You don't wake me up again, eh?
Remember?
House rules. No noises, 1 till 2.
Yes?
Quote? Quote?

JACK: 'When...when...' We haven't learned it yet,
sir.

SAMUEL: And you?

JAMES: 'When...when'...

SAMUEL: '...Master sleeps, none shall speak!
Life goes on, when Master wakes!!'
Eh?
Ha, ha, ha.
Learn, boys!

(Exit SAMUEL. Off-stage.)

Learn!
Learn!!

JACK: How can we behave like that!!!

JAMES: Fawning lick-spittles, aren't we really?

JACK: Aagh. Again, again!
           Knee bender!

           Promoter!

           Dingbat!

           Sapadilla!

JAMES: I don't know what you mean, Jack!
           Speak clearly!

(They turn away from each other, JACK tugging JAMES;
BILLY's mocking laughter, off-stage; enter BILLY,
creeping.)

BILLY: Ooh, you crawlers!
           Creepy crawlers, crabs!
           What are you after, eh?
           Sirring away! Got no guts, eh?
           He despises you, you know.
           You've picked it up quick, huh?
           Here five minutes, and there go your double
               tongues, darting in and out, duetting it!
           Phew! You're real characters!
           Two-backed beast!

(Thumbing):

           He calls you that.
           Behind your backs!
           Get that!

(Darting behind them):

           You've got two broad backs,
           For thwacks.
           They'll come,
           Dodge them, if you can!

(JACK and JAMES clinging to each other, lower their
heads.)

JACK: Coward!

BILLY: It's two against one, isn't it?
           Ha, ha!

JAMES: We're one!
           We're one! You're educated, Billy, you'll
                                        understand.

      We will have company to the end!
      We will die together!

(JACK covers his face.)

JACK: There's a real consolation for you, young Billy!

(Exit BILLY.)

JAMES: Think about that!
      We're not unnatural, Billy!
      There's no such thing. Don't you dare...

JACK: ...You can trust us, Billy.
      We will be true, Billy.

JAMES: We are one and company!
      So it's not bad at all, it's not bad really.

JACK: You're silent now, Billy.

JAMES: You ought to apologise to us, you ought!
      There are consolations for our state.
      We're not sorry!.
      What do you say to that? Eh?

(They look up. JAMES to JACK):

      We're not ashamed!
      We care for each other!

(They turn their heads opposite ways.)

      We are one, really!

SCENE FOUR

Some time later. The set is illuminated. It is a festive night,
for celebrants in SAMUEL's residence. It is his birthday.
The neighbours have come. The sounds of music and voices
from the next room. Three guests in evening dress totter
through the room, and out again. The sounds of music grow
louder. Applause. A speech is being made; the singing of
'Happy Birthday' is audible. In runs SAMUEL, clutching
glass, in tails, greying hair awry, puffing, pale. After
him spill the guests, among them MARTHA, and the house-
hold. BILLY and MILLY are in their party rig. There are
shouts of 'Where are the twins?' and 'Where are they?'
and 'Let's have 'em'.

VOICES: The twins!! Bring on the twins!

SAMUEL: No! No! My night!
Announcement! Me!
Silence! A chair!
Billy! Milly! Chair, chair!
I told you! Before.
Quick!

(A chair is brought by BILLY.)

VOICES: The twins!

SAMUEL: No! No! Me! Samuel speaks!

(He clambers onto the chair.)

Oh! Ah! Good!

(Applause.)

My good friends!
And citizens!
King Samuel speaks! Hear me!

You do me a great honour.
I welcome you to my board, with gladness in my
heart.

But I am not selfish.
Oh, no!

(Laughter.)

I want this to be somebody else's day, too! Why
not?
For what is happiness, if you cannot share it?
Tonight is also for another.

VOICES: Hear, hear!

(Laughter.)

SAMUEL: I have always loved my family, that you know.
To them is my first obligation.
Not to outsiders or guests or other persons.

Don't be ashamed of your Daddy, Billy!
He does his best, for an old man, a sick man,
So sick and tired.

I have no woman or wife to be my partner, that
you know already.

MARTHA: Shame!

SAMUEL: But I have tonight chosen a new companion.

MARTHA & OTHER VOICES:
Engaged, Sammy? Who? Who?

SAMUEL : Not engaged. You should know better.
What am I saying?
Tonight, a girl has become a new woman.
I decided.

(SAMUEL tries to get off his chair; he pushes MARTHA away.)

Billy! You naughty boy. Help your Daddy!

Ladies and gentlemen, I present you Milly!!

(He takes MILLIE's hand.)

Long live woman Milly!
She's a big girl now.
Look at her, people!
Isn't she beautiful?
Isn't she pretty?

(Cries of 'yes'.)

A real woman. Her mama would be proud of her,
Let us drink for Milly!

Speak Milly!
Speak to our guests!

VOICES: Go on Milly!

MILLY: It's your day father, not mine.
This is your birthday, King Samuel!

SAMUEL: Yes, yes! Go on! Go on!

MILLY: You are sovereign.

(SAMUEL mouths the words.)

None can share it with you.

BILLY: Your decisions are decrees...

SAMUEL: Yes, yes...

BILLY: ...And your generosity a legend in the realm...

...We do not wish to usurp you, in this your
capital city.

SAMUEL (clapping):
Bravo, bravo! Good!
Yes? Go on!

BILLY: Er...er...you...

SAMUEL: Yes?

BILLY: Er...I know that you...

SAMUEL: Forgotten, Billy, today of all days?
          This special day, different from all other days?

(BILLY covers his face; MILLY comforts him; BILLY
tears himself away, and runs out.)

          And you Milly, you comfort your lazy brother?
          You leave me lonely.
          Sure. She leaves me in the lurch.
          Like always.

          Do I have to call on outsiders? Eh?
          Them I can trust.
          I knew it!!
          They will be a lesson to you.
          All of you!
          They will remember! Eh?
          They will do their duty,
          My will will be done!

(Laughter. He claps his hands.)

          Enter!
          Jack and James!
          Here is your moment!!
          For all time, teach them a lesson!

VOICES: The twins!

SAMUEL: Yes! 'The twins'!
          So what? Are they a peepshow for you?
          Is this a circus, or something?
          You should be ashamed.
          You mind their feelings.

(To MILLY):

          Ah, now you come! Maybe I fail, but I try Milly,
                                        my little daughter.

(MILLY takes SAMUEL's hand. JACK and JAMES enter,
silken-clothed, powdered-white-faced, full-wigged, one
also wearing a feathered hat and smoking a clay-pipe, the
other holding a tankard and wearing spectacles. Applause.)

SAMUEL

          Welcome, strangers!
          I greet you among my subjects.
          My home is my capital!
          My estate my country!
          My income, my revenue!
          It is all at your disposal!

(JAMES drinks to him. They advance in step, with a fixed

> smile, and practised gesture.)

JACK: Long live...

JAMES: ...The King!

JACK: Long may...

JAMES: ...He reign!

JACK: Samuel...

JAMES: ...Oh Samuel!!

> (They begin to dance; the music grows louder.)

SAMUEL: All dance! Dance!!!

ALL (including SAMUEL):
> Samuel, oh Samuel,
> Samuel, my dear!

> (SAMUEL links on to JACK and JAMES, a dance a trois: JACK and JAMES perfectly in step, SAMUEL out of step.)

> Praises be upon your head,
> In this your sixtieth year!

> (Applause from all, including SAMUEL.)

SAMUEL: You see, all of you? Do you see?
> Not a single slip in their tongues,
> Word-perfect, even.
> My true two friends! My two true friends!
> I announce to you a great idea. Listen, friends!
> > You also.
> This we didn't think of before. Too bad.
> And why? I should know! We go through all the
> > rooms, eh? The congo!

> We do the congo!!

JACK: Singing?

JAMES: And dancing?

SAMUEL: Good boys! You...you...
> ...Cotton on quick.
> Yes!! Two heads are better than one!
> Heh, heh! Good old Sammy!
> The boys have a great idea!!
> Let's go!! Music!

> (They form up, leaving MILLY.)

> Come Milly. Join! At the end!

ALL: 'Samuel, oh Samuel,

> Samuel, my dear!
> Samuel, my dear!
> Praises be upon your pate
> In this your sixtieth year!
>
> Samuel, oh Samuel,
> Samuel, my dear,
> Shit upon you and your state,
> In this your sixtieth year!'

(Exeunt, singing and shouting. Off-stage the sounds of tramping, breaking glass, laughter and singing. MILLY is left alone; she dabs her eyes and looks in a mirror.)

SAMUEL (off-stage):
> Milly! Milly!

(Enter SAMUEL, running.)

> Milly, you don't join in. Why?
> Why not?!

MILLY: Father!

SAMUEL: I know! Don't say!
> You're ashamed, like Billy! Ashamed of your father.
> In my own home! I should care!
> It's good here, isn't it?
> Do you lack something?
> Food, shelter, what?

MILLY: Those poor boys, poor Jack, poor James.

SAMUEL: You're sorry for them, eh?
> You like them, eh?

(He grabs her arm.)

> Pity, love, which?
> Tell me! Listen to me when I speak!
> Shall I tell you something?
> I...despise them!!!
> Yes!!
> Lick-spittles! Cringers! Slaves!!

(Roaring):

> Have they no dignity? They have no dignity!!
> I can see it, Milly!
> You must be proud in this world.
> They have no pride.
> They do all I say, everything.
> They learn the rules,
> They follow me.

> They praise me! Ugh!
> Me! Old Sammy!
> Who am I to be praised!
> But you, Milly.
> You're different.
> I can trust you.
> You have spirit. And Billy!
>
> People should have spirit.
> That's what all people truly believe.
> No spirit, no soul!

(He seizes her by the scruff of her neck.)

> Be a rebel, Milly!
> While you can.
> You agree? Can you hear me?
> You do?
> Good!
> Then you and I can be friends,
> Trusty friends, flesh and blood, please,

(Swaying):

> Your father, Milly. Here I am!

(The procession breaks in, JACK and JAMES at the head. All sing as before, one or two pairs kissing and struggling.)

Two people pull at JACK and JAMES, wonderingly. JAMES has his arm round a woman, JACK trying to free them.)

> They compete, Milly! Kissing now.
> Oh! They even kiss!!

(JAMES kisses a woman's cheek.)

> You see that!
> Disgusting! Ah! Playing!
> You see that! So deep!
> Disgusting!! Help me!

(SAMUEL retches, mouth agape; he runs off shouting. Off-stage):

> Help me!

(MILLY watches and takes a step towards the guests.)

SCENE FIVE

The bedroom of JACK and JAMES. Bed double, chair double,
coat-hanger double, and so forth. The sparsest set: a few
possessions: a photograph of themselves.

They enter, tired, their collars open at the necks.

A weak table-lamp burns. A distant shouting voice of
SAMUEL, his words inaudible.

They sit down heavily on the bed. They both yawn and
stretch. They take off their joint-jacket together. They
toss it away.

They rest their heads against each other.
One takes the other's hand, slowly.
They don't look at each other. Their faces are expressionless.

They remain thus for a few seconds.
With resignation, and patience, they struggle up and kick off
their shoes, fumble with their trousers, which they take off
with ease. They toss them away.

They stand in their shirt tails. They bend down simultaneously
to take off their socks. One makes to go one way, the other
the other.

They sit down on the bed again.

JACK moves abruptly, pulling JAMES, as he twists round to
draw back the bed-covers. JAMES stops him, and pulls out
the chamber pot from beneath the bed, offering it to JACK.
JACK shakes his head.

They both yawn again.
They clamber, awkwardly and strenuously, into the bed.
JACK switches off the light.

SCENE SIX

After the party, the guests gone. The sounds of giggling female
laughter, creaking, a man's grunts, and soft music are heard.

SAMUEL, the petitioner, is desperately wooing MARTHA.
She is befurred, over-painted, grotesquely coquettish. The
two struggle at, and over, a sofa.

MARTHA, queening it, laughingly fobs off SAMUEL.

MARTHA   Sammy, you silly boy!
              Get up Sammy! And such a party!
              Your grown-up daughter,

        Sammy!
        She's coming.

SAMUEL: Martha, please! I implore you.

MARTHA (pulling him closer):
        No, Sammy!
        No, Sammy! You're the limit!

(She kisses him voraciously, and strokes his pate.)

        No, I will not!!

        Billy, where's Billy?
        Oh, god!
        What will they say?
        You're a disgrace, Sammy!
        You ought to be ashamed.

SAMUEL (beaming):
        I'm a man, Martha.
        I shock myself!
        Oo I do! Whee!

        Mm! Mouths full of kisses.

MARTHA: No!
        You take liberties with a defenceless woman,
                       Sammy: a widow!

(She shudders.)

        An old man!
        Old!!! Sammy!
        Do you know?

        You're old and grey and tired, Sammy!
        And look at you!

(SAMUEL looks at himself.)

        Acting like a boy!
        Like a young boy!
        Like Billy, your own boy, Billy.

(She straightens her dress. SAMUEL clambers to his feet.
MARTHA begins to make up. SAMUEL turns away.)

        You slushy man.
        You've been alone too long, Sammy.
        You should find yourself a nice woman again.

SAMUEL: You, Martha?

MARTHA: No, Sammy.

        I'm too...nothing for you.
        You're a big man, Sammy. You always were.
        Big ideas, big dreams.

SAMUEL: Yes?

MARTHA: I understand, mind you.

SAMUEL: You do?!

MARTHA: Of course.
        You're a lovely man, Sammy.
        You're proud.
        A nice home. I've got to go now.

(Taking up her coat):

        Comfort, security.
        Good children. Help me.
        Generous.
        You...you...do good things.

(Whispering):

        You take in strangers.
        You pity the sick and the lame. It doesn't matter
                         to Sammy. Not to Sammy.
        Everybody says so, everybody.
        They talk. They beging to talk.
        Why do you do it, Sammy, they say?
        What's the point? It isn't normal.
        You tell your Martha, hm?

SAMUEL: What's the point?
        You can ask me that?
        You can be so simple, Martha?
        You feel nothing? Eh?

        Oh dear, oh dear!
        I'm a human, aren't I?
        Am I a man?!
        Have I a mind of my own?
        Will you deny it?
        Here is the world, Martha!
        All life is here!
        It's good, Martha! It's good! Don't you see?

(He scratches.)

        My visions grow. Boundless! Luscious!
        My mind creates. Beauties! Pregnant!

MARTHA: Pregnant?!! All this talking. I've got to go now.

SAMUEL: Samuel, the King!
I make order from chaos.
For the good of all.
I see all the flux of life.
I choose.
The natural and the unnatural.
The pure and the monstrous...

MARTHA: Bye-bye, Sammy.

SAMUEL: The single, the joined.
In the unnatural, shall true nature be seen!

(Exit MARTHA, unseen.)

Samuel knows.
Of course, Martha, there are many anxieties for
a man like me, who thinks.
Problems.
Dark pains.

Not pains like you understand,
Martha.
Dark ones.

(Tapping head):

In here, where they hurt me.
Why do we have two eyes, when one will do?
Dark pains.

(He sits down. A long pause; he sees she has gone.)

Always uncertain!! Mind in flux!!
I don't care!!
I don't care!! Why should I care?

(Enter BILLY. He sniffs the perfumed air. SAMUEL belches.
BILLY winces.)

BILLY: Feeling sorry for yourself, again,
Samuel? Not so...festive any longer?

(A silence.)

Feeling sorry for yourself?

SAMUEL: Yes, Billy.
You might say that.
You might say that, a young boy like you.

BILLY: I'm not the only one.
We all do. We're always saying it!!
What else is there to do in this ruddy place?

What else...

SAMUEL: ...All of you?

BILLY: Yeah. Sure.

SAMUEL: Jack? James?

BILLY: They? Sure.
            All of us. 'All the family!' The whole fucking
                                                outfit.

SAMUEL: Jack and James?

BILLY: Course! What do you expect?

SAMUEL: You're lying again, swearing.

BILLY: Well I was, so what? We're frustrated! Can't
                                        you see, Dad?
            People who are frustrated say anything.
            You must have done once, when you were young.
            Milly and I are thinking of going away!
            We are! We've had enough of this life.
            You're just a tyrant!
            Milly says you're a small-town dictator; she says
                    you're a provincial, and a...a...vulg...

SAMUEL: A vulgarian?

    (SAMUEL gets up.)

BILLY: No.

SAMUEL: A vulgar man?

BILLY: No!

SAMUEL: A vulgarian?

BILLY: Look! No! I told you!

SAMUEL: Milly says I'm a vulgar man, uh?

    (SAMUEL grabs hold of BILLY's arm.)

BILLY: No!

    (BILLY draws away violently.)

SAMUEL: You're lying again.

BILLY: Yes, dad.

SAMUEL: Billy!

BILLY: You can't reach me, father.
            It's too late, I'm afraid.

> We've missed our chance, the two of us.
> It'll never be any different now.
>
> Childhood is over for me.
> I feel it, dad.
> I think it.
>
> You don't know me any more.

SAMUEL: You don't know me, Billy.
           Don't you care about that?

BILLY: No.

SAMUEL: Go then.
           Get out then!!!
           GET OUT!!

   (JACK and JAMES enter, running trouserless.
   SAMUEL, panting, hand on heart.)

BILLY: I will.
           I'll be glad to.
           You'll be sorry, later.
           Then, what'll you do?
           Your only son.
           You'd have those bleeding monsters instead,
                                      wouldn't you?
           Those freaks!!
           You want to play with 'em like toys.
           They flatter you. People come to see them.
           You feel popular.
           Star of the show!
           What about them?
           The poor crippled, twisted, unnatural, bastards.
           You prefer them.
           You'd see us go, wouldn't you?

SAMUEL: Get out!

BILLY: And Milly too, eh?

SAMUEL: No. Not Milly.
           You're alone.

   (JACK and JAMES join BILLY. JAMES takes him by the arm.
   BILLY does not respond.)

BILLY: You can't make me.
           I have rights.

   (SAMUEL belches, and belches and scratches.)

SAMUEL: You want to stay with this...and this!

This ugliness!
You so refined, so cultivated, Billy.
How can you stand it?
With your taste!

Childhood is over.
You're a man, Billy, sure. I envy you.
Tonight you can go forth, my son.

He'll search the universe, the sun, the moon and
                    the stars. Oh my god, he will!
Such a man!
Look at you!
He wants to join the world! Tee, hee.
Where's he going? Eh? I ask you!

(BILLY begins to move away. To JACK and JAMES):

Can he know?
Does he know? Eh, boys?
This child!
I can't reach him. Sammy, the King, can't reach
                                            him!

So what? Eh?
So what?
Does it matter?
Do I care? Do you have the insolence to think I
                                            care?

No.
My consolations, boys, are infinite.
My world is whole.
Children, you are free.
You are all free to come, and to go, together, not
                                        together.

Remember me, forget me.

(He pirouettes, even dances. To JACK and JAMES):
Split up if you like, eh?
...Spoil this home,
Find another...
...Don't find another...
We create it all, so what difference, boys?
My thoughts are more real than all of you put to-
                                        gether...

...or separate.
Whatever you wish.

(A pause, BILLY moves a step away again.)

> And so I go to bed. You also, boys.

(A silence.)

> I have enough to live on!!

(JAMES looks at BILLY; JACK turns to JAMES, but find him
occupied.)

> I, Samuel!
> Look at me! Look at me, Billy!!

(BILLY leaves, JACK and JAMES trying to restrain him.)

SCENE SEVEN

Later, MILLY in pyjamas, sits dishevelled, tearful, on the flo
JACK and JAMES, in shirts as before, stand looking at her.

MILLY: Poor Billy!
            What will happen to him? What will happen?

JACK: ...He'll be all right.

(JACK and JAMES sit down near her.)

JAMES: He can look after himself.
            He'll be all right, Milly, you'll see.

JACK: He can look after himself, can't he?

MILLY: It's easy for you to talk. It's different for you..
            ...I'm sorry. I didn't mean that.

(She crouches before them, resting her head on JACK's kne

> You're so gentle and comforting.
> Both of you, each of you.
> But sometimes I don't think of you as two boys.
> > Isn't that funny?
> You're both so gentle and good.
> But ... but ...
>
> ... Hey ... can you both feel it when my head's
> > resting here?
>
> If I do this ...

(She runs her hand up JACK's leg.)

> ... Does it tickle you both?

Eh? Go on, tell me.
Don't sulk, I don't mind, anything.
Tell me.

If I ... kissed ... one of you, would it be exciting,
oh, all round, you know, eh?
Tell me, tell me! Please!!

Prudes!
You are shy!

I love you more and more.
You sit like little joined birds, scared, don't you?

Ashamed of yourselves.
Why should you be?
You're young and strong and handsome.
Don't be shy!
I'm your Milly! Aren't I?
I know all about you, so there!
Boo!

I've seen ... everything!!

(They turn apart.)

You don't know, but I have.
After all, I do for you, don't I?
I clean and tidy and wash.
And ... I see everything.
I know more than the others.
I understand.
You haven't any secrets from your Milly.
Oh no, not a single little hidden secret.

(She clasps JACK's legs to her.)

Not one.
It makes me happy.
It does.

I'm not sorry for you.
You're not thinking that, are you?
I'm not, I'm not!!
Don't think that! don't, don't!!
You mustn't!

It's not true, it's not true.
Don't believe him if he said it.
Daddy lies. He always lies.
Billy's gone now. Everything's breaking.

> I can feel it.
> Will he be all right?
> It's Daddy. I can't trust him any longer.

(Crying out):

> He says, 'Aren't you disgusted with those poor
> boys, Milly?'
> Oh, oh!
> Don't listen to what I say.
> I say the wrong thing.
> I never know what I mean.
> I think the right things, but I never say them.
> Help me boys! Please!

(JAMES deftly puts his arm round her, drawing her towards him.)

> You're lucky!
> That's what I think.
> My silly head's all on its own, isn't it? ...
> ... Inside, there's only me.
> But you can ... you can share all your thoughts,
> can't you

(JAMES' hand strays over MILLY.)

> I mean ... sort of ... pool them.
> So you've got ... so if you have ideas you can sor
> them out, and pool them and discuss them, and the
> decide what to do, can't y

(JACK begins to tremble.)

> You can have the same memories and plans, and if
> you're not sure what to do you can put your heads
> together and decide, and it's not so bad if you
> make mistakes, is it? and if you see lovely things
> you never feel, oh, I wish someone was here to
> share it, like I do, and you can ...

(JACK wrenches himself to his feet dragging JAMES with him

JACK: ... No!! No!! No!!
          No!!

(He darts round dragging JAMES.)

> Stop! Stop!!
> You've got it wrong!
> Don't mock us! Oh! Don't mock us!

(JAMES takes hold of MILLY, fondling her; JACK begins to

struggle with him.)

> Fool!
> Madman!!
> See how she mocks you! See! See!!

(JAMES kisses her frenziedly.)

MILLY: Which of you did that to me?!

(They both groan.)

> Which? Which?
> You apologise to me!!
> No one's ever done that to me before.
> You've taken something from me!
> Me! Milly!
> To do a thing like that.
> When ... I thought ... we were like sister and
> > brother.

> To let me down!
> I thought you were different from other people.
> I did! I did! Honestly!

> You did it, James! You!

JACK: I did it.
It was me!

MILLY: How could you?

(Backing away.)

> How could you despise me so?

> Boys like you.

JACK: I don't know ...

JAMES: ... What came over us!

JACK: A sudden ...

JAMES: ... Passion!!

JACK: We rarely ...

JAMES: ... Get the chance.
Sex is hard to come by.

JACK: No privacy ...

JAMES: ... For one ...

JACK: ... What we see! ...

(They dance.)

JAMES: ... What we see!

JACK: ... Or t'other ...

JAMES: ... Eyes ...

JACK: ... Eyes ...
             ... Everywhere.
             All that's left ...

JAMES: ... Is a quick kiss ...

JACK: ... For a beautiful girl.

JAMES: Like you ...

(They both kiss her on the cheek.)

JACK: We're looking for two ...

JAMES: ... Like us, Milly ...

JACK: ... We're on the hunt ...

JAMES: In fact, we travel the whole world, truly ...

JACK and JAMES:
             ... In our desperate hunts,
             For two joined ...

(MILLY giggles.)

JACK: ... c ... c ... creatures ...
             ... with whom ...

JAMES: ... We can sate ourselves ...

JACK: ... And play ...

             ... The four-backed beast!!!

JAMES: ... And have ...

JACK: ... Two families.

JAMES: Two lots of little children ...

(They both mop their eyes.)

JACK: ...Running...

JAMES: ...About...

JACK: ...All...

JAMES: ...Over!

(They both, laugh, together, mouths wide.)

MILLY: Aaah!
            Sweet creatures!

JAMES: Still friends?

(MILLY nestles against JAMES, head on his shoulder. His hands stray; she stops nothing.)

MILLY: Naughty boy!

(JAMES and JACK move like automata, fondling her in turn.)

            Devil!
            Ooh!
            Don't!
            Oh!
            What are you doing?!!
            No!
            No!!

(A knocking from above.)

SAMUEL (voice off-stage distant):
            Milly! Bed!! Milly!

(Another clumping knock.)

            To bed! Go to bed!!
            Milly!

MILLY: I must go now.
            King Samuel calls!

JACK (with hatred):
            King Samuel!!!
            Ha, ha, ha!
            What a game!
            What a farce!

JAMES (gently):
            Milly! Your daddy calls.
            Don't be so silly!

JACK: Be proud, James, be proud!

JAMES: Oh, ah, ah! Oh, Jacko!

(JACK wrenches him fiercely.)

            Why are you doing that? Tell me, Jacko,
            Tell me!

JACK (with fury):
            King Samuel!! God save our gracious King!!
            Sing, sing in a cage!!

MILLY: Poor father!
How you deceive him!
Poor old man! Sick and sleeping.
His generosity, and you mock him so.
How can you!
How dare you! In his room, behind his back, to m
his Milly!
After what you've done to his own Milly,
Pawing me, mauling me.

Shouldn't I tell him?
Eh?

JACK (to JAMES): Silly old bugger!
Crackpot dreamer!

JAMES: Don't, don't Jacko!

JACK: Vulgarian!!
Farting belcher!!
Belching farter!!

(MILLY springs at him, and slaps his cheeck; they both reco
JACK pulling JAMES with him.)

MILLY: You wait!
You frauds!
Just getting what you can out of innocent people!
Using people,
Exploiting them.
Making people pity you!
I pity you all right.
Who wouldn't?!
We all do!! We all do!!!
Do you hear?
Everything's going wrong!
Poor house!
Poor room!
Poor things!
You've made it ugly.
We've come too near you. Ugh!

I'm just a girl, can't you see?
You tried to lead me on, didn't you?
Beasts!!
I'm just a girl, can't you see?

(A pause. She runs out.)

JACK: Bad scheme of life for me!

JAMES: Take it easy, Jacko!

JACK: Bad scheme, bad scheme!

JAMES: Be grateful, be grateful at least.

JACK: For what, exactly?

JAMES: Young tits?

JACK (crying out):
             Aaah!

JAMES (dancing round, dragging JACK):
             Good chances here, boy!
             Did you see the way she ...

JACK: ... Stop!!

JAMES: I'm grateful, yes, grateful, Jacko!
             For a place, a refuge, a pair of ...

JACK: ... Don't underestimate me, brother!
             Speak for yourself only.
             Let's be honest now, shall we?

JAMES: Have you nothing better to offer?

JACK: How about you, hm?
             I've everything to offer. So much!!!

JAMES (rubbing his thighs):
             I've got a lot too, at the moment.

JACK: No! Enough!

(He turns away from JAMES.)

JAMES (pressing face close to JACK):
             Or is it a 'mind of your own' you want to show us
                                                          all?

             Is that it, brother?
             The old dream?
             Hm?

             And compassion, pity, understanding, love, com-
             passion, pity, understanding, love ... ?
             Are you offering those too?

(JACK hits him hard; JAMES doubles up forcing JACK down,
part way.)

JAMES: You're a better man than me.
             It makes it hard for you, dragging me around like
                                                          this.

(Putting his arm round JACK):

> Poor you!
> We're popular together, though, aren't we?

JACK: I suppose so.

JAMES: Aren't we?

JACK: Maybe.

JAMES: We are.

JACK: Yes, brother.

JAMES: They envy us.
                    Here.

JACK: Maybe.

JAMES: They do.

JACK: Yes.

JAMES: They ...

JACK: I envy them, James!
                    Can't you understand?!

JAMES: Aah.
                    I knew.

JACK: I envy them their ... beauty.

JAMES: She certainly can ...

JACK: ... do you see the way they move, and run, James
                    They can be alone,
                    Go free and single, oh,
                    Minds of their own...

JAMES (afraid):
> ... I told you, I told you ...

(JACK hops round, pulling JAMES.)

JACK: ... Sovereign,
                    Sovereigns ...

JAMES: King Samuel!!!

JACK: ...An open world,
                    Each to his own path,
                    Oh, and what are we...?

JAMES: ...Misshapen beasts? Eh?
                    Is that it?

JACK: No, James.
           Two men, like I always said.

JAMES: We're not, we're not.
           Don't say it.
           We think the same, say the same.
           Eh, eh? Don't we?
           I got in your way, is that it?
           You want to kill me?
           Eh? Get me out of the way?
           Is that it?

JACK: Don't be afraid, James.
           We act our parts, don't we?

JAMES: Yes, we do. If you say ...

JACK: ... We mustn't. We must set out alone, search for ...

JAMES: ... But ...

JACK: ... Keep to ourselves,
           Think to ourselves,
           Be ourselves ...

JAMES: ... Jack! Jack! What is it, Jack?
           What are you saying, what are you saying?

JACK: Let our separate visions grow! Let our lives ...

JAMES: ... It's only words, Jack.
           Let me, let me share your life, Jack. I'm nothing.

JACK: No more.

JAMES: No more?
           But we need to, don't we?
           I can't go away, Jack.
           I would if I could, for you.

JAMES: I can't, can I?
           Oh Jack!

JACK: It's what I mean.
           It's what I mean, at last.
           Don't mistake me any more, James.

JAMES: It'll never be the same, then?

JACK: No.

(JAMES giggles stupidly, then hysterically.)

JAMES (tugging):
           We're still together, aren't we?

Oh yes.
It's all there.
How about Milly?
Eh? That touch, that ...

JACK: ... You want her body, don't you?

JAMES: Don't you, Jack?

JACK: No!

JAMES: No?
Those thighs, those ...

JACK: ... No!!!
We're obscene to her, brother!

JAMES: She said ...

JACK: ... Never mind what she said.
We nauseate her, brother!

JAMES: We do? We don't!!
I don't nauseate her, Jacko.

JACK: Wouldn't you...like me out of the way
then?

JAMES: No!
How could you think that?

(Off-stage distant voices, male and female.)

I suppose she's not that good, Jacko!

(A girl crying: SAMUEL shouting 'whore' and 'slut'.)

Other birds, other tails!
Knock-around broads!

(MILLY enters dressed to leave, with a case; JACK sees her,
not JAMES.)

Hunks of hat!
Little twidgets for Jimmy!
On the road again.

MILLY: I'll leave it all to you, boys!

Me too! First Billy, now me!
That's it, look innocent!
You've done it!
Nothing left here, for us! His Billy and Milly!

I love him.

He doesn't know. I love him.
He'll never know.
You can tell him. Tête-à-tête.
How about that?
Carry the news. Ugh!

(JAMES tries to move to her, but JACK remains rooted.)

JAMES: Oh dear, oh dear!

MILLY: He 'begins to believe in you!'
Now he says it!
How about that?
Not us. Oh no. Not his Billy and Milly!
'Poor boys!' 'They'll never know anything differ-
                                        ent!' 'I pity them.'
'Their own world.'
'Think of it.' 'What a mystery,' he says.
A mystery!
You've got a friend up there.
You use him!

JAMES: Poor Milly! Poor Billy!
And you?

MILLY: Ah, me!
At last!
Me! Eh?
Don't bother your heads about me!
Oh, no!
You've had your fill of me, haven't you?

(They both shake their heads.)

MILLY: A single thought!
One mind with a single thought!

'Milly,
You egged them on,' he says.
'They wouldn't do that.'
'King Samuel decrees you to be a whore!'
'It's a shame!
A disgusting thing in my house.'
Can I reply?
How unjust! Can I speak?
'You have no case.'
No case!!!

It's all breaking, boys.
We leave it all to you.

(JAMES strains to move: JACK stays firm. Twirling about):

> I'm moving now.
> Watch me move!
> See me go!
> See us scatter!
> Billy, Milly!
> Bye-bye, Milly!

(JAMES drags JACK a few feet. Exit MILLY. A silence.)

JACK: Be proud!

JAMES: Be proud?!

JACK: Must get away! Must!

JAMES: Yes! Let's go ...

(JAMES makes to go. JACK stands his ground.)

JACK: ... Disown all tears!

JAMES: Dis ... ?

JACK: Hide!

JAMES: Hide?

JACK (pulling away):
>   It's all breaking!

JAMES: Not us!
>   Not us!
>   I don't care about them more than you.
>   I don't!!
>   I don't! She's not that good, Jacko!

JACK: You don't!
>   You're lying, eh?
>   To console me! You'd say anything for my sake,
>   eh?
>   You'd compromise, would you?

(Banging off-stage.)

>   You believe in nothing!
>   That's your trouble.
>   Nothing to cling to.
>   Only me! Blindly!

JAMES: It's not true. No!

JACK: A dead weight.
>   That's all you are!
>   A dead weight!!

JAMES: I don't give a damn for you.

(Terrified):

           There! If you want to know.

JACK: That's it then.
           Nor I for you, James!!

(JAMES tries to stop him going on.)

           Nor I for you!!

(They look fleetingly at each other. They tug in opposite directions.)

           You can have your Milly!
           You go one way, me another!

JAMES: You bet!
           You bet!
           Glory, glory, glory!!!

JACK: Nothing to fall back on!
           Alone!
           No cheap pity, James!
           It's all over!

JAMES: Oh yes! Yes!

   (SAMUEL runs in.)

SAMUEL: Boys, boys!!!

JACK: To join ...

JAMES: ... the movement, eh?...

JACK: ... of the world!!

JAMES: To help her ... Milly ...

JACK: Nothing ...

   (They fall to the ground.)

SAMUEL: Oh, boys! Harmony! Please! Stay with me!!

JAMES: ... To fear!

(They are on their knees, facing apart, and pulling apart.)

JACK: Two men!

SAMUEL: Don't boys! Oi!

        Sammy's alone!

JAMES: Don't, Jacko!

JACK: Two men!

(They break apart.)

        James, James! Help me!

SAMUEL: You've ruined it all!!!
        Stay together! Boys!
        All fallen!
        Samuel is alone!

        Billy! Milly!! Billy!

(JACK and JAMES stand up, and run off in separate directions.)

Act Two

SCENE ONE

Some time later.
SAMUEL, older, is standing in his room, as in Act One, Scene
One.
But all is shabby, soiled.
He is motionless, eyes downcast.
He is unkempt, shirt awry, collar-less, pale.
He is holding up his trousers with both hands.
His discarded clothing lies on the floor.
As the scene begins, SAMUEL momentarily darts a glance towards
the audience; then turns his back on them.
He is trembling, perhaps weeping.

A silence.

SAMUEL: Oh.
Is Samuel here?
Samuel...is still...here.
The dirty games are finished.

(To audience):

    You can go!

(Quickly):

    Carrion!!

    Here was Samuel, the King!!
Lord of his long lived-in domain.

(He pulls at his own hair.)

    Ugh!

(He plucks contemptuously at any object to hand.)

    All touched.

(He sniffs the object, clutching his trousers with free hand.)

    All soiled.
Beasts have been here.
Here...beasts have been.
May they burn to ash,
Cinder their souls!!
Samuel will have no pity.

(He pulls at his own hair, and then examines his fist. Trembling.)

    Wisps.

Dust.
Dusty hair.
Blue lips.
Old man!

Get out, people!
Go home!
The dirty games are over.
Nothing for you to stay for.
Carrion!

(A silence.)

Only an old man, soiled, is left.
Alone.
The stink and shame of it for me,
Samuel, prince of men!

(He lets go of his trousers, arms at his sides.)

Samuel, father and friend!

(His trousers begin to descend. He clutches at them, ashame

But him you shall not have.
Samuel is not for you.
That I shall deny you.
I ask nothing.
I give you nothing which is mine.
My poor body you shall not have,
Carrion!!

(A silence.)

Who have I to thank for this and this?
Children, lovers, friends!
May they wander alone to the ends of the world,
And far beyond, outcasts!
May their bodies rot!
May their breaths smell to the heavens, of sin!

(A silence.)

Samuel...will have no pity.
My flesh and blood would do this?
To think...
...If I had dreamed...
...To any human person...
...With my heart...

(A silence.)

Here beasts sat. Yes.

The unclean in a pure house.
I opened the door for Elijah,
And let in beasts. So.
Oh my god!
Forgive Samuel.
Ugh!
Here they sat, soiling my place!!
Strangers! Here!!
May they burn to ash,
For the ruin of my house!!
Yes!!
Now I see!

The first spot here.
Here they stood.

(He scrabbles on the ground, sniffing and scraping.)

The contagion.
Like lepers.
Soiling, seaming,
From here to here.
And here.
Smell!
A trace! A spot!
A drop!
Ugh!!
So be it on Samuel's head!!
So be it! My sin too, my sin!

(He sits down. A silence.)

Still, Samuel is free.
Here he sits, a free man.
That I still have.
Here I can dream.

(He tries to brush the chair in which he sits with his hand, as
if to tidy it. A silence.)

Silly Samuel!
Silly boy!
I...use...bad words.
I...say bad things,
My fellow-men.
Is that a sin,
When they curse me?

Can I ask my flesh and blood to rot?
Have I come to this?

They deserve it.
They had it coming.
Samuel must have no pity.

Look at me!

(He stands up.)

They must crawl for forgiveness,
Here, on their knees, to this spot,
And beg!!!
Then, maybe.
If they don't?
Huh!
So what? Should I worry?
Samuel is free,
Me they will not have!

(A pause.)

I cannot afford to be alone.

(He cocks his ear.)

Maybe they come now, eh?
Already.
Billy, Milly!
Martha! Pah!
Martha, little Martha.

(He smiles.)

Forgiveness, a few arguments, I told you so's,
                                etcetera, etceter
All together. A real family. Hm?
A new foot to start.
A few heads around me. Life.
Good things.
They come? What?

(He sits down.)

No. No. Ah. Esau wept, but too late.
I will be better. A better man.
I cannot afford.
Now Samuel knows the ropes.
I will be better. Sure. Easy.

They will come to me.
Samuel in his bones, he knows the truth!
All the world is here.
Here they must come.

Where else have they got, I ask you?
And who else?

(A pause.)

I know. They will come.
They have no strength to stay alone.
Billy, Milly, Martha.
Sammy knows.
Do I want them?
Maybe, maybe not.
They will come.

(He cocks an ear again. He chuckles.)

SCENE TWO

A fairground booth: A crowd clustering about. Fairground music, hubbub, the rhythmic shrieks of girls on the Big Dipper. Cries and laughter, inside the booth and out. This is JAMES' stall: with photographs of himself on the wall of the booth, alone, and with JACK.

JAMES, a stump of arm wrapped in coloured flounce, and silk-shirted, regales a small group, mostly of women.

Tittering laughter and guffaws.

JAMES leers, and slaps his thigh.

JAMES: Oh ladies and gentlemen, it's true, it's true ...
           ... The things we saw!
           You wouldn't believe it, honest!
           My gawd! Ladies, I've got a real beauty ... for you
                                        ... next! Come on, luv!

           Come on in.

           One night ... this beautiful bint ...

(He describes her with his hands.)

           ... Oooh! real good stuff ... she comes to me ...
           she says 'how about a bit, eh, cocky?' ... you should
           have seen Jack's face!!...

(He bends double, the crowd laughs, though he doesn't.)

           Can we be alone, she sez?!!
           Ha, ha, ha, oh, oh.

Alone!! I ask you!
Me and her. Oooh!
'Tell him to take himself off!
And we can have a little hanky-wanky-panky!'

(Laughter.)

Right, I says, to Jack, that'll come in handy!

(Laughter.)

How about moving off? Eh?
I've got a date, Jacko, I sez.
Fair's fair.
Fair do's.
I bloody will not, he sez.
I can't!!
'Yer can't?
Go on, you daft bugger'...she sez.
'Where there's a will, there's a way!'
So you know what he sez?

(Cries of 'no'.)

He says ... he says ... I'll close me eyes.
And get it over quick. I arsk you, ladies and
                                    gentlemen
'Get it over quick.' The jealous thing!

A big job like that, too.
A strong fella like me.

(Laughter.)

Just imagine it, ladies.
Anyway I won't go into details.

('Aaah.')

Not with the gentlemen here.
No! Well, I don't want to embarrass them, you kn
                                    how it i

(A pause.)

A WOMAN: Did he shut his eyes, Jimmy?

JAMES: Thank you for asking that question, luv!
          Did he shut his eyes?
          Did he shut his eyes?!!!

          He did not!
          He saw the lot!
          We were very close!

I was attached to my brother.

(Applause and laughter, led by the questioner.)

Very.
Mind you, he was to me, too.
Don't get me wrong!

(A pause.)

And now, ladies and gentlemen, to finish off, I'll
leave you with a little song, specially composed
for my visit – and let me say how glad I am to have
been able to have this little talk with you, by ...
ahem...myself – and set to music by my friend
Harry here.

Harry!
Where the hell are you'arry?
Wind the bloody thing up, 'Arry boy!

(Enter fat HARRY, with an accordion.)

Give him a hand, ladies!

(Applause.)

Where've you been, 'Arry boy?
Morning sickness again, eh?

(Laughter.)

He looks well on it, though, don't you think?
It's not his fault.
People take advantage of him.
He's soft. Let's 'em all come!!

(Laughter.)

HARRY: What's it to be, boss?

JAMES: He speaks!
           Give him a big hand!

(Laughter and applause.)

Good old 'Arry!
You're not as daft as you look!

HARRY: Boss!

JAMES: He's upset!
           Aaaah!

ALL: Aaaah! Aaaah!

(JAMES mops his eyes: some of the crowd do too.)

          What...a...shame!!

(Laughter.)

JAMES: Silence, folks!
                Leave the victim alone.

(Aside):

          He doesn't deserve it.
          Give me a 'C' Harry!

(A sound is emitted, flat.)

          Be serious Harry!
          They're paying for this.
          The suckers!!

(A better sound.)

          One...two...go!

(Singing.)

            'Once upon an 'orrible time,
            But not so long ago,
            You wouldn't have recognised me, friends,
            You wouldn't have known me, oh no, no,
            You wouldn't have known me, no.

(A collecting box is carried round, being shaken vigorously.

            Cos James and Jack –
            And this is a fact
            Were tied to one another,
            And we were low, we were so low,
            You wouldn't have known me, oh, no, no,
            You wouldn't have known Jack, either.

(One or two depart, as the collecting box approaches them.)

            Thank you, thank you, folks.
            So I sez to him, one fine fine day –
            'Why don't we find our fortunes?
            Brother Jack, you go one way,
            And I'll go in the other,
            Oh I'll go in the other'.

(Most leave.)

            So we struggled in a chosen place,
            Trying to break our fierce embrace,
            We struggled and struggled, ladies and gents –

(The lady questioner tidies up and gives HARRY the collecti

box; she leaves.)

> And then it happened, oh so quick,
> Our partnership went down the nick,
>
> And I was one and he the other,
> And he was on and I the other.

> Now I come to the...

(HARRY stops playing.)

HARRY: ...Boss!

JAMES: Oh yes.
Thank you, Harry.
I've got a lousy voice, haven't I,
Harry?

HARRY: Yes, boss.

JAMES: How much today?

(HARRY weighs the box in his hand, as he hands it over to JAMES.)

HARRY: About four, maybe less, maybe more.

JAMES: Not bad, eh? Have a day off tomorrow eh, Harry
boy? We'll have a breather.

(HARRY dismantles the booth.)

> This mob'll take anything, won't they?
> Any old smut.
> They smile and grin, don't they
> Harry?

(Wagging his stump.)

> They like a bit of filth.
> A spot o' the monster stuff.
> Makes 'em feel better, doesn't it Harry? Eh?

> They don't think of us, do they?
> Where we've come from.
> Where we're going.
> Just summat to smirk at.
> That'll do 'em fine.

(All signs identifying the booth as JAMES' have been put away.)

> Still, Harry boy.
> We've got the right formula for 'em,

As you might say.

(Giving HARRY the box):

The cash rolls in.
Eh? boy?

What are you complaining about, then?

HARRY: I'm not complaining. It's you.

JAMES: I'm not complaining.
I like it here.
It's great.

(Crying out):

Who's complaining?

(Exit JAMES. HARRY opens the collecting box, and furtively
picks out a certain amount. He pockets what he has taken and
sighs. Enter JACK, one armed, carrying his pack or bag.)

JACK: Good day to you, sir.

HARRY: Yes. Oh.

(JACK stops.)

JACK: What courtesy!

HARRY: You a city chap then?

JACK: Not particularly, no.

HARRY: And what does that mean?
Begging your pardon, o' course.

JACK: Not at all, not at all.

HARRY: Just takin' the air, hem?

JACK: Exactly.
I'm looking around.

HARRY: Good fair.
Big Dipper.
Listen.

What've you done ... with that arm o' yours then?

JACK: That's a personal matter,
No offence but ...

HARRY: You bin in the wars, eh?
You a foreigner by any chance?

JACK: A stranger.

That's all.
Looking round.

HARRY: You a refugee?
Eh?
Running away?

Come on, let's have it.
None o' this fancy-nancy-malarkey, and all.
Let's have it straight!

JACK: Just a minute, just a minute.

HARRY: Man to man!

JACK: Be polite, be polite!

HARRY: Get on with it then.
We haven't got all night, mate.
Say yer bloody say, and let's have done.
Ha, ha, ha!

JACK: You'd take advantage of a crippled man, wandering
alone ...

HARRY: ... Don't make me cry, Jack ...

JACK: Jack?

HARRY: Come on!!
Out with it!!
What d'you want round here?
What are you putting your bloody nose in for?
I got my bloody living to think of
Without you coming here and buggering me up?
Get out with you!
I got the formula. We stick together.
Me and him. Don't you go ...

JACK: ... There must be some mistake.
Come, sir.
We're both men of the world.
Free and equal ... Let's ...

HARRY: ... It's all right, pal, I'm not scared of you or
anything,
You and your soft-mouth squit.
It confuses a fella like me,
Giving me the pap.
Let me go,
I don't feel well.
Me weight and all. Look at me, so pasty.

> Out of breath. A 'uman 'ulk.
> I got me wife and kids.
> Must get back.
> You know.
> Sorry if I've been rude.
> It wasn't meant.

JACK: A moment, please.

HARRY: There's nothing for a gent like you,
> In a place like this.
> If I were you, I'd keep... moving on.
> Us fairground folk are a rough bunch.
> Ta – ta!
> That's it.
> Eh?

JACK: My brother's here.

HARRY: No.

(A pause.)

> We could team up! You and me!
> Eh?

(HARRY clutches JACK's sleeve. JACK shakes him off.)

> What about me?
> Where would I fit in?
> Three's no good!
> I got me wife and kids. I got...

JACK: ...He's here.
> You lied.

(A pause.)

HARRY: Yeh.

(HARRY giggles, stuffing hand to mouth.)

SCENE THREE

Some time later. It is evening. A dim light. JACK's humble
house, where he sits reading swathed in black silks, spectacle
The room is sparse, bare. A wooden table, with a water jug
and a single glass. JAMES enters in coloured clothes, a tum-

bler, with a small jingling bag, tired.
He empties out the contents, which cascade on to the table. The
coins roll on the floor.
JAMES grins.
JACK is disturbed from his reading and, expressionless, gazes
at him.

JACK: How much, brother James?

JAMES: Twelve, I reckon.

JACK: How much did you give Harry?

JAMES: 'Arry got the usual.
             Two.
             Two, that's all! Don't worry!!
             I remembered what you said!

JACK: Don't raise the voice, brother James!
             There's a good fellow. Hm?

JAMES: Aah!

  (JACK reads on.)

             You could be more generous, couldn't you?

JACK: With Harry?!

JAMES: With me.

JACK:

             With you?!
             We understand each other, don't we?
             You've got what you want, haven't you, eh?

             Company...a roof...something to do, I suppose.

  (JACK returns to reading.)

JAMES: I'm lonely, Jack.
             Should I be?
             What do you think?
             Eh?

             I'm selling tales, like a hack,
             Like a...whore.
             Aren't I, Jacko?
             Is it right?
             Should I be?

JACK: You chose it, didn't you?

JAMES: Should I be, should I be?

JACK: Stop whimpering!
             You couldn't drag me down for ever!

JAMES: Oh Jack.

JACK: Let me get on with this, there's a good fellow.

(A silence. JAMES sits down on edge of JACK's chair.)

JAMES: I understand you, you know.
             I know how you think.
             I mean, I know how I think, so...

JACK: ...So?

JAMES: So...so it's OK, isn't it Jack?

(JAMES stands up.)

             I can count on you.
             Comforting me. I mean...

             ...I love you!!

(A silence.)

             I accept all you say.
             I mean you've turned out cleverer than me.
             You've got the ideas...for both of us, haven't y

(Taking JACK's hand):

             Share them, please share with me!

JACK: The same old drivel, eh?
             Nothing's changed with you.

JAMES: I can't argue.
             I'm tired.

(JAMES sits down.)

JACK: It is only a matter of effort.
             Be ascetic.
             Be pure!
             Garner ideas!
             Thoughts more real than ourselves.
             I'd salute your visions, if you had any.
             Make poems in the mind.
             Think, inwardly question, inwardly answer.

JAMES: Yes. Yes. Oh dear.
             What about Sammy?
             There's a question! Isn't it, Jacko?

(JAMES giggles.)

Sammy!
Poor Sammy!
Alone.

JACK: He can cope.
I can.
He can! You can, if your try.
There was nothing there for you.

JAMES: Yes. No.

(JACK springs up, and fiercely grabs hold of JAMES, dragging him to his feet.)

JACK: We're swimming alone!!
Free of all that. It was stale,
James, stale!
The tide roars round us two!

JAMES: No, no! Please!

JACK: We're engulfed!

JAMES (as if drowning):
No! No!

JACK (as if holding JAMES up in rescue):
Strike out!
Thresh about!
Swim, boy, swim!!
Take to the stream!
Don't go down!

JAMES (clinging to Jack's neck):
Oh!
Don't frighten me, Jack!
I don't like it.
I can't swim.

Liar, liar! Cheat!
We can't swim!!!
So there, so there!
You can't do anything I can't do.
You never learned.
Remember?
We never picked up that trick, did we, eh?
Book-expert!
That's all you are.
'Swim, boy, swim!'

Look at you!!

(He comes close to JACK and touches his shoulder.)

That arm's like mine, isn't it, Jacko? Monster
boy!!!

(JACK strikes him fiercely. JAMES laughs.)

JACK: Don't call me Jacko!

JAMES: I'm still close to you, aren't I?
           Jacko?

JACK: Get away from me!
           Don't you dare touch me!!

JAMES: I won't touch you.
           Don't be afraid!
           I won't spoil your progress!

           But I want to tell you something.
           I've been thinking.
           Not like you, Jacko. Oh no. Of course not.
           But I have been thinking all the same.

           You'll listen, won't you?
           Harry agrees with me too, Jacko.
           He says you're trying to use me.
           Now I don't think that. I'm your real brother now
           I wouldn't go that far. Oh no.
           But you're very clever, Jacko.
           You want to improve yourself, don't you?
           That's what I think.

           I know, I know, don't protest.
           But I go out to work, Jacko, don't I?
           I go on my own.
           That's not very nice for me, is it?
           I can't spend my time 'making poems in my mind'

           That's not for James really, is it?
           Mind you, don't under-estimate me.

(Tapping head):

           I've got a few things there too.
           But I shan't tell you.
           Well, I go out, don't I? I see a bit.
           You told me to, didn't you?
           What d'you expect?

           You said we'll 'have a little partnership'.
           'We'll have our own targets, we'll go our own w
                            like we planned from the
           And I've been working with Harry, and you've b
                                     here

        Don't get me wrong. I'll do it for you.
        Because you're much cleverer than James.
        I'm not looking for all the grand things like you.
        I'm carnal, aren't I?!!

        That's what you call me.
        You think, and I act, eh?

(Giggling to himself):

        Between the two of us, Jacko...
        ... We'd make a decent sort of man, wouldn't we?
        That's what I think.
        Harry does too.
        You see, I don't think much of myself on my own,
        but you – you're everything I'd like to be, Jacko.
        Oh yes.
        I like what you've got.
        It sort of attracts me.
        And ... I've got some things you could ...

(JACK turns away.)

        ... Don't be angry, Jacko!
        We're brothers aren't we, proper brothers now?
        I don't want to get in your way.
        Don't be afraid of that.
        I can be a help to you now, Jacko.
        I've seen a lot now, on my own.
        But I want to share it with you!!
        I want to share our lives!

        Can't you see? I love you!
        Eh?

JACK: Oh, no, no!
        What are you saying?

JAMES (tugging JACK's sleeve):
        I can see what I like in you.
        I mean ... the things I haven't got.
        Don't make me say this, Jack.
        Can't you see?

JACK: Ugh! Get away from me!
        Get away!!

JAMES: You can mock me now!
        Can't you?
        Now you'll make fun. Won't you? You're doing
        something. I don't understand it now. Tell me!

> You're leaving me behind.
> You've got ideas.
> What are they? Tell me!

(JAMES clutches at JACK again and falls down.)

> Where are you going?

(JACK moves and drags JAMES.)

> You're dragging me.
> Like before, Jacko, like before.
> Isn't it, isn't it?
> We are one, we are, we are!!

(JACK groans and drags JAMES again.)

> We should never have done it, never.
> It was Sammy's fault, wasn't it?

> It's what he wanted. I knew all the time.

(JACK kicks him away.)

> I could see it coming. I never warned you, did I?
> Could you see it coming, Jacko?
> Could you see it too?

JACK: Get up James.
Get up!

(JACK extends his hand and pulls him up; then touches JAMES
stump gently.)

> We understand one another, don't we?
> Ye...es, of course we do.
> Give me something to drink.
> Go on, quickly.

JAMES: Yes, Jack, yes!

(He scurries to the table, pours a glass of water.)

> Here's your drink, Jacko.
> Is it good?
> Is it good?
> Eh?
> Look at me.
> Look at me!!
> Do you remember me, Jacko?

JACK: Yes, I remember.

JAMES (dancing around JACK):
Say it better, say it better!

JACK: What?

JAMES: Mean it, mean it!!

JACK: I mean it.
           Of course I mean it.

JAMES: What do you remember?
           What do you remember?
           Eh, eh?

JACK: The times we spent together.

JAMES: You do, you do!

JACK: I do.

JAMES: You preferred the old times?
           You did? Didn't you? Eh?

JACK: No, James.

JAMES: Why not?
           Couldn't you?
           We have the...same memories, don't we?
           Eh, Jacko, eh?
           How d'you get round that?
           Aha!
           Answer that!

           We saw the same, didn't we?
           We did the same? Eh?
           We moved the same,
           We ate the same,
           We loved the same,
           We thought the same.

(Tapping JACK's forehead.)

           We think the same,
           Oh, ah, we do, we do still, don't deny it, Jimmy
               knows, you can't fool your Jimmy, never, never,
               never, just you try, just you try...

JACK: ...James!!

(JACK lashes out.)

           Enough!...

JAMES (tweaking JACK's nose):
               ...Not enough, no!
           We lived together,
           We slept together,
           We were born together, weren't we, eh?

Harry says you're using me and you won't stand
       by me any more. We talk about it.
He says 'Jimmy boy, you wanna watch 'im'. Tha
       how he talks, poor old fat Harry.

(JACK sits down.)

He says 'you'll kill yourself with all this work,
And what thanks do you get?' None, I said.
He made me think about it, Jacko.
He's my friend, now.
I told him. I said...

JACK: ...Poor James!
           Poor boy!

JAMES: Don't try that line with me!!
           That won't work.
           You won't get round me like tha.
           You have to work things out with me, really.
                            don't you?
           You know that.
           I see it in your eyes, when I come close.
           You have to think things out with me.
           Eh?
           Like we always did.
           But...but...
           You don't go out, like I do!
           You stay here.
           You hide, Jacko.
           Don't hide, Jacko.
           I go in crowds on my own.
           I see things different now.
           You don't know what I'm finding out, do you?
           You don't go out,
           For all your talk.
           You're lonely aren't you, boy?

JACK: ...Don't call me boy!

JAMES: ...No more getting cross.
           You just listen to me!
           You daren't go out!!

JACK: I dare.

JAMES: You dare, you dare!
           What would you do?
           With your bad arm,
           And your big ideas!
           Ha, ha!

You're...caught!!

(Beginning to pursue JACK):

      You don't like me touching you any more.
      Think of all those people,
      Milling around you.
      The stalls, the cries, the raucous yells,
      The smell, the leering mouths,
      The meats, and flies...think, think, Jacko...

      ...The painted girls, the furs and cloths,
      The sweat, the dust, ugh!...
      ...The lust, the groans, the roaring noise,
      The lights, the heat, the cold...
      Ugh, ugh!
      Think, think, Jacko!
      That's where I go. Me! James!
      Your James!

(JACK covers his face.)

JACK: No! No!

JAMES: You don't like the sound of it, do you?
      I didn't think you would!
      It was better once, wasn't it?
      You weren't lonely then.
      We had the best company, didn't we?
      Love, warmth, a place, eh?
      Remember? Remember poor Sammy's place,
      Eh?

(A pause. With furious energy he drags JACK to his feet.)

      Dance, dance, like the old times!
      Dance to..gether!!
      One...two, one...two!
      On! On! Ha!
      Jack and James,
      James and Jack,
      Back to back,
      Wha, ha, ha!
      One...two, one...two,
      One...two, one...two,
      Dance, dance, like the old times!
      Dance together!!
      One two, one two,
      One two, one two,
      On! On! On! On!

SCENE FOUR

SAMUEL's room, feminized. Some time later. MARTHA is in-
stalled in it, varnishing her nails, slippered, hair in a net. A
perfumed odour. She has chocolates; she puts one into her mou
She wears a wedding ring. She has a lipsticked cup of coffee by
her, on a gracious table. She has a cast-aside magazine. She i
content. She takes up the magazine, reads, grins, tuts, lays it
aside, examines her nails, sniffs her coffee, and feels the cup.
She raises her head, with an idea.

MARTHA: Sa..a..mmy! Here a minute!
     Sammy! Martha wants you!
     Ah! Where is the man?
     He never comes any more! It's a disgrace! I wast
                 my breath! So soo
     So soon!
     What's the matter with you, Sammy?

     Billy!!
     Your mama wants you!
     Oh, a scandal. Those kids! So soon!!!
     Milly!!
     Milly!!!

     They don't respect me!
     And why not? Eh? Why not?

(Exit MARTHA. Off-stage):

     What thanks do I get for it? Sa...mmy!

(Enter SAMUEL, aged. He finds a chocolate on the floor, and
eats it. He is about to examine MARTHA's magazine, when th
door begins to open: he withdraws from MARTHA's things.
Enter BILLY, older.)

SAMUEL: Ah, Billy! Good! Where's Martha?

(MARTHA, off-stage, calls.)

BILLY: Don't look so guilty!
     You don't have to be so...polite, do you?

     You asked for it. You wanted her.

SAMUEL: She's your mother now. Respect her.
     And don't discuss it with me!

BILLY: All right, all right! Have it your way!
     If you're so afraid.

(Exit BILLY. MARTHA, off-stage, calls. Enter MARTHA.)

MARTHA: Everywhere I've been, looking for you.
                Naughty Sammy!
                I ask you. Where are you?

(He pats her on the arm.)

                You pat me, eh?

(He puts his arm round her.)

                You tell me nothing. I've been calling my lungs
                                                out.

(He kisses her cheek.)

                And what thanks do I get from any of you?

SAMUEL: Aah, Martha! Darling!
                You're upset again, aren't you?
                The children get on top of you.
                I know, I know.
                I understand. I think we should...

MARTHA: ...You're so polite, Sammy! So polite!
                What's the matter with you?
                You don't speak normal to me any more!
                You go all hoity-toity with me!
                I'm your Martha. Don't you recognize me no more,
                                    or something?
                Sammy! Come to me, Sammy!

(He doesn't move.)

                You don't love me Sammy, do you?
                That's the real truth! Isn't it, Samuel?
                Now you've got me, you don't care any longer!
                          Oh! What a tragedy!
                Ah, let Martha do it. She can wash and cook and
                                      slave.
                A fat lot you care! A...fat...lot...you...care!!
                Didn't I come here and make things nice, eh?

                Look at you, Sammy!
                I'm proud of you. Clean, smart, a real man!
                I stopped all your nonsense.
                Oh yes, didn't I?
                Sure I did!

> I got you in the nip of time, let me tell you!
> Where would you be now? I ask you!
> Eh?
> Where?
> No mother for Billy and Milly!
> Don't you ever think for one minute?
> Where would you be? '
> All your crazy ideas running round the house!
>
> Rotting away here. No woman. Nothing.
> No lovey-dovey...no koochi-koo...
> Where would you be, Sammy?

(Touching him):

> You know you like me, really.

(She puts her arms round him from behind.)

> Sa...mmy! Your little Oomphy's here!
> Aaah! Isn't that nice?

SAMUEL: Yes Martha, yes!

MARTHA: There!! Course it is! Silly Sammy!

SAMUEL: I'm sorry, Ooomphy!
> Darling! Here's your Sammy!
> Course he loves you!
> Take me Martha!
> Take me!
> I'm selfish.

(They kiss.)

> Mmm.
> I'm cruel to you, aren't I?

MARTHA: You are, Samuel.

(They embrace.)

SAMUEL: I hurt you, don't I?

MARTHA: No longer, Sammy.

SAMUEL: You're happy.

MARTHA: Yes. And you?

SAMUEL: Of course I am, Martha, darling.

MARTHA: You getting polite with me again, Samuel?

SAMUEL: Of course not. How could you think it?

MARTHA: How could I think it?
            Oh, Sammy!
            Is that the way to talk to a wife?

SAMUEL: What way?

MARTHA: That way!

SAMUEL: I'm not aware of anything.

MARTHA: That way, Sammy!
            You're doing it again. Oh dear, oh dear!
            That it should happen to me!
            Me, Martha! Did I deserve it?

(She flops down. SAMUEL turns away.)

SAMUEL: You're too...quick for me – by a long chalk!

MARTHA: Too quick? What is this quick?
            A long chalk! Such treatment from a man!
            'Long chalk, long chalk' 'Too quick'.
            Listen to him!

(She furtively discovers a chocolate.)

SAMUEL (scratching):
            Ah, you make me feel...weary.
            If you want to know.
            We waste all our precious time together!

            What for? Eh?
            What example is it to Milly and Billy? You tell me!
                                              Go on!
            As if they weren't bad enough! Ugh!

            The cowards!
            Spineless, spunkless!!
            That Billy! That pimpled weakling!
            That simpering spoiled girl! Ugh!

(She stands up.)

            To think of it!
            No guts! No courage!
            Do they ever risk anything, try anything?
            Do they? Eh? Answer me!!
            Oh, oh!
            How I tried!!
            Go on, stare!
            Ugh! These disgusting chocolates!!

(He stamps on one.)

    Yes, go on! What do they get from you, eh?
    Have a good cry! So what?
    I don't care! I'm sick of it.
    The whole works!

(Scratching):

    What have they done with their lives?
    Eh? Do you know?
    Ah? What?
    That it should happen here!
    What pride can I have? You tell me!
    Why do I ask you? Nah.
    What's the point?

(To himself):

    Once...just once...I thought...maybe, this is it.
                                    At last.
    They're going to do something. Milly and Billy.
    Venture a little.
    Be bold. Dare to be wise.
    Try a little.
    Move...away.
    A man and a woman.

    Everybody would say 'There's Sammy's example
                     for you. Chips off the block.'
    They would, Martha. I'm telling you.
    'Nice independent kiddies you got, Samuel!'

    And what did they do? I ask you, what did they do?
    'I'm not staying here another second.
    And don't you try to find me either!'
    'You're a tyrant, that's what you are!
    I despise you!!'
    They despise me, they!

    And then?
    They go!! Gone!
    And then? After a while, what happens?
    They come back.

    Oh!
    So you laugh.
    You laugh, eh?

(To audience):

> She laughs!
> A fine thing.
> For my plans.
> My own children should turn out this way.
> What a sad surrender!

MARTHA: Sammy!
Sad surrender, sad surrender!
What's the matter with you?
You can say that, a father?

SAMUEL: Aah!
They fill the air with their excuses.
Always the make excuses.
'We have learned a lot, Daddy.'
'It changed us going away, honestly.'
So weak! So empty! Aagh!
They cry!
They love me!
They miss me!
Always so sad!
Sad to see me old.
Sad to see me grey.
They feel sad. I should worry!
It's me should feel sad, eh Martha?

Fancy!
What can I do?
So I get old. So what?
I must apologize because they feel sad, eh?

MARTHA: They're only children, Sammy.
You're a big man.

(Eating a chocolate):

> Don't be hard on them.
> Do they know things like you?
> Can they think things out like you?
> Don't be a slave-driver, Sammy!
> They love you. That's what counts.
> They want to be near you!

(SAMUEL groans.)

> Sammy!
> I revolt you, Samuel. Eh?

SAMUEL: No, no!
Don't I learn, find out, imagine, try, wander stil
Eh? Don't I?

MARTHA: Oh, Sammy, I don't know what you're talking
about.

SAMUEL: Don't I soar like a bird?

(He flaps his arms: she stops him.)

In here? Still?

(He scratches.)

MARTHA: Like a bird?

SAMUEL (clutching MARTHA's hand):
Don't I make order here?

MARTHA: Oh yes, plenty.
That you do all right.
Come, lie down a bit, Sammy.

SAMUEL: For the good of all. You don't realise.
I had new ideas. Plans. So many.
I've waited all this time.
I wanted to talk to them.

(Whispering):

Jack and James.
I could have done it with them.
Good boys! Poor creatures. An example.

MARTHA: Yes, Sammy!

SAMUEL: They'll never come back, will they?
Brave boys!
What they did!
Oh god!

(He is led to the sofa, and is made to sit down.)

MARTHA: There! Stretch out. That's it.

SAMUEL: No, no.

(She puts his limbs into arrangement.)

MARTHA: Good boy! Nice?
Comfy? There!

SAMUEL: Oh, oh.

MARTHA: I get you a nice cup of tea, eh?
You have a few winks, eh?
Martha'll get you a nice drink.

(Exit MARTHA.)

SAMUEL (eyes closed):
You don't know what they did, Martha.
No. Better that way. You didn't see.
I was witness. Good old Samuel!
I was there. On the spot.
As usual.

(A pause. He struggles up onto his elbow, looks round, sees he is alone, and gains strength.)

Didn't I try?
To stop them. What could I do, eh?
Bad move they made. Terrible pain.
Ugh!
Jack and James.

(Lying back):

They will not come back to me. No.

(The door opens slowly.)

The flux of the world has swept them away.

(Enter MILLY, now a comfortable woman, and BILLY.)

Far away. Who knows?
They loved each other.
That Samuel could see.

(They approach on tip-toe.)

Poor Milly.
Did she worship them!
And Billy.
Jealous! Of those poor fellows!

A small man. That's why.
A nothing, really.
Milly? Just a girl, that's all.
What do you expect? Why worry?

A good wife: and finish.
A shame mind you.
Tch! To think.

(A pause.)

But those boys! My!

What a pair! Fan...tas...tic!
How they cared for each other!
Interesting fellas, mind you.
Makes you think.
What a life!
They liked me. That I could see.
Absolutely.
In my house anybody is welcome.
The sick, the crazy... even the deformed.

(He giggles.)

Why not?
What do I lose?

Sure they were individuals.
One was one, and the other the other.
Sure.
Normal guys! Ask Milly!
What do you want for your money?
That they should be something special?
Ah!

They wanted to go.
So good luck to them!
Is it my responsibility?
Here they had a place. What more can I do?

Not good enough, maybe. Not enough fun, not en
this, not enough that.
Not enough life. Who knows?
That's their business.

I understand. Yes, I understand.
Basically, I understand... sure.
Sammy sees.
What is there here for boys like them?
Eh?
Only Sammy. So what?

(Sitting up.)

Who's Sammy, to them?

My ideas! What are they?
Nothing. Second-hand goods.
Maybe if we'd talked together.
Who knows?

(A pause.)

And my kids?

                    Pah!
                    They wanted the world. They!

(He raises his head and listens. Off-stage, the sound of rattling plates.)

                    For them, isn't it all here?
                    I ask you!

(Enter MARTHA with tea-tray; SAMUEL, without looking round, quickly lies back, eyes closed.)

MARTHA: Milly!
                    Billy !

(SAMUEL leaps off the sofa and spins round.)

                    Where've you been?
                    You don't come when I call!
                    Nothing!
                    Help your mama, Billy!

SAMUEL (grabbing MILLY):
                    How long?!
                    What are you doing?
                    How long have you been here?
                    Eh?

MILLY: Ow! Get off me!
                    You've bruised my arm!

BILLY: We've just come in this second.
                    Take it easy.
                    Don't get so excited all the time.

MARTHA: Billy!

MILLY: Why do you want to know, Daddy?

SAMUEL: I want to know.
                    Can't I know?!

BILLY: Talking in your sleep?

SAMUEL: You should say a thing like that?

(He seizes a piece of cake and eats noisily, choking.)

MARTHA: Samuel! Sssh! Be careful.

(MARTHA gives him a plate. MILLY and BILLY laugh.)

SAMUEL: Quiet!! Quiet!
                    How dare you!

(He hurls the plate to the ground, and stamps on it.)

> In my own house!
> Get out!
> GET OUT!!
> In future I, Samuel, eat alone!!

(SAMUEL advances on BILLY: MARTHA tries to restrain SAMUEL.)

> You pigs!!

MARTHA: Go on kiddies, Daddy's angry. Run along. Sammy
says...try to...understand.
> Billy! Please!!

(SAMUEL takes hold of BILLY; BILLY strikes back; SAMUEL stumbles and almost falls; MARTHA goes to his aid. He regain his balance himself. MARTHA sobs, MILLY sees a spectacle BILLY stands his ground.)

BILLY: ...And who's Sammy?
Hm?
What makes you so sure you understand us, eh?
With your ideas.
What are they?
Nothing!
Second-hand goods, eh Sammy?

> Don't be afraid of me!
> I'm only a small man.
> I'm not an interesting fella, am I?

(Grasping SAMUEL by the lapel.)

> Eh?

> Not like those strays you picked up somewhere.
> To feed your curiosity.
> To indulge yourself with.
> Those bloody deformed animals!

(He pulls SAMUEL to him; then pushes him away.)

MARTHA: Billy!

BILLY: Now they've left, it's OK with you isn't it Sammy
Out of sight, out of mind.
It's enough for you that they were brave.
That's the limit of your sympathy, isn't it?
A bit of curiosity.

> A diversion.
> 'The last word in entertainment...full of diverting
possibilities, the two-backed be

    Eh, Sammy? Remember?
    Quite a sensation, weren't they?
    But what went wrong?
    They didn't fall for you did they, somehow?
    Very strange.
    They wanted to get away.
    You're not surprised, are you?
    Of course not. You understood them.
    So good luck to them!

(BILLY leads MILLY away.)

    They're not your responsibility, after all.
    What more could you do?
    Ah, wash your hands of them. Get it over!
    At least they haven't come back!
    They're not cowards.

(MARTHA wipes her eyes.)

    They have each other, haven't they?

    They went away together, so why worry?
    The flux of the world has swept them away.
    They'll earn a living, won't they?
    The two-backed beast!
    They made a good act for you, at any rate.
    They'll earn, they'll earn!
    Don't worry!

(BILLY and MILLY go out, leaving the door open. A long
silence.)

SAMUEL (whispering):
    Was that Billy, Martha?

MARTHA: Sure it was your Billy!
    Who else?

(She picks up the broken pieces of crockery. A long silence.)

SAMUEL (whispering):

    My Billy! My Billy!!

MARTHA: There!
    Aren't you proud of him?

SAMUEL: A sensible boy!

(He takes her hand. They giggle together.)

    A chip off the block!

SCENE FIVE

Anywhere. No set.
Enter, running, good arms entwined, JACK and JAMES, both in
coloured clothes, seeming more alike physically than at any pre-
vious time; nimbly moving in step from right to left, silently.
JACK stops in his tracks.

JACK: How do I look?
                Won't...Harry laugh?

JAMES

                Of course not...

  (JACK makes as if to bolt.)

                No, Jack.
                There's no point, Jack.

  (Enter HARRY, with accordion, with a balloon attached.)

HARRY: We got a great show tonight for 'em, eh fellas?
                And Jackie!
                Where is he?
                Where's the boy!
                There he is, there he is!

  (HARRY pushes the bad sides of JACK and JAMES together.)

                Watch this last number, boys!
                We wanna real climax, really moving, got me?
                We wanna round the bloody show off with a real
                                    bang, eh, lads!

  (They dance, he appraising, tapping a tune out. To JACK):

                We'll get you moving, won't we Jimmy lad?
                We'll polish you up, get you weavin', just like
                          your sexy brother. Heh-heh.
                Beau...tiful. There ain't no difference really.
                Keep at it, boys! It's coming!
                The public'll go for this.

  (A pause, HARRY tapping the time with his foot.)

                One-two, one-two, one-two...
                Take it from there, boys!

JAMES (singing):
                ...With a one-two, one-two, one-two,
                Hurrah for the double-backed beast!

JACK and JAMES (singing and dancing):
                For Jack and James are together –
                O why have we stayed together? –
                For ever and ever!

> With a one-two, one-two, one-two,
> Hurrah for the double-backed beast!

(They break apart, dancing.)

JAMES (singing):
> Sammy's alone
> And we're together...

HARRY:
> ...Keep to the script, boys,
> Keep to it...

JACK:
> No!
> Not alone!
> They'll all be together!

HARRY:
> Now then, now then,
> Keep to the script, boys!
> Watch it. Watch it Jacko!

(HARRY forces them together; they dance, JAMES dragging JACK.)

JAMES: And thank our lucky stars above...

HARRY: ...Sing, you bastard! Sing!

JAMES:
> That we have got each other,
> While far away,
> A kindly soul,
> Has lost his whole...dominion...

JACK: ...No!...

HARRY:
> ...Faster, faster!
> On, on, on!

(JACK and JAMES nimbly dance.)

JAMES:
> We joined the world,
> He hoped we'd be,
> Quite separate from each other...

(JACK and JAMES dance on, ignoring HARRY.)

> ...With a one-two, one-two, one-two,
> Hurrah for the double-backed beast!

JACK:
> We joined the world,
> To suffer and see,
> We joined the world,
> To think and be ...

> Quite separate from each other!

(They dance together, coming apart, linking their good arms, HARRY frantic.)

> With a one-two, one-two, one-two,
> Hurrah for the double backed beast!

(They begin to dance off, high-kicking can-can style.)

> With a one-two, one-two, one-two,
> Hurrah for the double-backed beast!
> Now Jack and James are together,
> For ever and ever!!
> With a one-two, one-two, one-two,
> Hurr-ah for...the...double...backed beast!!

(Exeunt, dancing, HARRY following, his balloon bursting as he waves goodbye.)

METHUEN'S MODERN PLAYS

Edited by John Cullen

Paul Ableman	GREEN JULIA
Jean Anouilh	ANTIGONE BECKET POOR BITOS RING ROUND THE MOON THE LARK THE REHEARSAL THE FIGHTING COCK
John Arden	SERJEANT MUSGRAVE'S DANCE THE WORKHOUSE DONKEY ARMSTRONG'S LAST GOODNIGHT LEFT-HANDED LIBERTY SOLDIER, SOLDIER and other plays
John Arden and Margaretta D'Arcy	THE BUSINESS OF GOOD GOVERNMENT THE ROYAL PARDON THE HERO RISES UP
Brendan Behan	THE QUARE FELLOW THE HOSTAGE
Edward Bond	SAVED NARROW ROAD TO THE DEEP NORTH
John Bowen	LITTLE BOXES THE DISORDERLY WOMEN
Bertolt Brecht	MOTHER COURAGE THE CAUCASIAN CHALK CIRCLE THE GOOD PERSON OF SZECHWAN THE LIFE OF GALILEO
Shelagh Delaney	A TASTE OF HONEY THE LION IN LOVE

Max Frisch	THE FIRE RAISERS ANDORRA
Jean Giraudoux	TIGER AT THE GATES DUEL OF ANGELS
Rolf Hochhuth	THE REPRESENTATIVE
Heinar Kipphardt	IN THE MATTER OF J. ROBERT OPPENHEIMER
Arthur Kopit	CHAMBER MUSIC and other plays
Jakov Lind	THE SILVER FOXES ARE DEAD and other plays
Henry Livings	EH?
John Mortimer	TWO STARS FOR COMFORT THE JUDGE
Joe Orton	CRIMES OF PASSION LOOT WHAT THE BUTLER SAW
Harold Pinter	THE BIRTHDAY PARTY THE ROOM and THE DUMB WAITER THE CARETAKER A SLIGHT ACHE and other plays THE COLLECTION and THE LOVER THE HOMECOMING TEA PARTY and other plays LANDSCAPE and SILENCE
Jean-Paul Sartre	CRIME PASSIONNEL
Theatre Workshop and Charles Chilton	OH WHAT A LOVELY WAR